EXPLORING THE SUBATOMIC WORLD

Understanding
NEUTRONS

B. H. Fields
and Fred Bortz

Cavendish
Square

New York

To Susan, who long ago set off a chain reaction for me.

Published in 2016 by Cavendish Square Publishing, LLC
243 5th Avenue, Suite 136, New York, NY 10016

First Edition

Website: cavendishsq.com

This publication represents the opinions and views of the author based on his or her personal experience, knowledge, and research. The information in this book serves as a general guide only. The author and publisher have used their best efforts in preparing this book and disclaim liability rising directly or indirectly from the use and application of this book.

CPSIA Compliance Information: Batch #WS15CSQ

All websites were available and accurate when this book was sent to press.

Library of Congress Cataloging-in-Publication Data

Fields, B. H., author.
Understanding neutrons / B.H. Fields and Fred Bortz.
pages cm — (Exploring the subatomic world)
Includes bibliographical references and index.
ISBN 978-1-50260-542-9 (hardcover) ISBN 978-1-50260-543-6 (ebook)
1. Neutrons—Juvenile literature. 2. Particles (Nuclear physics)—Juvenile literature.
I. Bortz, Fred, 1944- author. II. Title. III. Series: Exploring the subatomic world.

QC793.5.N462F48 2015
539.7'213—dc23

2014049225

Editorial Director: David McNamara
Editor: Andrew Coddington
Copy Editor: Cynthia Roby
Art Director: Jeffrey Talbot
Designer: Stephanie Flecha
Senior Production Manager: Jennifer Ryder-Talbot
Production Editor: Renni Johnson
Photo Research: J8 Media

The photographs in this book are used by permission and through the courtesy of: nobeastsofierce/iStock/Thinkstock, cover and throughout; File:Aristotle in Thomas Stanley History of Philosophy.jpg/Wikimedia Commons, 7; Ann Ronan Pictures/Print Collector/Getty Images, 8; Ann Ronan Pictures/Print Collector/Getty Images, 11; Public Domain/File:Joseph Louis Gay-Lussac.jpg/Wikimedia Commons, 12; Public Domain/File:Менд.jpg/Wikimedia Commons, 14; Thomas Forget, 15; SSPL/Getty Images, 17; Library of Congress/File:Ernest Rutherford 1908.jpg/Wikimedia Commons, 19; Public Domain/File:PSM V56 D0024 J J Thompson.png/Wikimedia Commons, 20; Thomas Forget, 24; Thomas Forget, 26, 28–29; Public Domain/Smithsonian Institution/File:Enrico Fermi at the blackboard.jpg/Wikimedia Commons, 31; Thomas Forget, 33; Roger Viollet/Getty Images, 35; Thomas Forget, 36, 39, 42; Public Domain/File:Otto Hahn und Lise Meitner.jpg/Wikimedia Commons, 44; Dorling Kindersley/Getty Images, 47; Vector version by Dake with English labels by Papa Lima Whiskey, lines modified by Mfield/File:Gun-type fission weapon multilang thin lines.svg/Wikimedia Commons, 48; Yoshikazu Tsuno/AFP/Getty Images, 50; American Stock Archive/Archive Photos/Getty Images, 52–53; Martin Lisner/Shutterstock.com, 54.

Printed in the United States of America

Contents

Authors' Note

Readers of the entire Exploring the Subatomic World series will notice many similarities between this book and *Understanding Protons*. That is unavoidable. To physicists such as myself, the proton and the neutron are two different aspects of the same particle that we sometimes call the nucleon. The historical aspects of their stories are quite similar, and thus many parts of the two books are also nearly the same. But there are significant differences between the books as well. I hope you will use both the similarities and differences to understand both types of nucleon and to appreciate what that understanding means to science and technology.

Introduction

All matter is made of **atoms**. That statement may seem obvious to you, but when English chemist John Dalton (1766–1844) made that statement in 1803, it transformed science.

Yet Dalton's idea was far from new. The ancient Greek philosophers Leucippus and Democritus had suggested it twenty-three centuries earlier when they asked themselves how small they could cut a piece of matter without changing its nature. They described the smallest possible piece as *atomos*, meaning indivisible. But their ideas were only of the mind, while Dalton connected the notion of atoms to laboratory observations.

In Dalton's theory, the smallest pieces of most substances turn out not to be atoms but **molecules**. A water molecule is made of two hydrogen atoms and one oxygen atom (H_2O). Thus it is not indivisible, but it is still the smallest speck of matter that can still be called water. Dalton spoke of two kinds of substances: elements, which are made of only one kind of atom; and compounds, which are made of only one kind of molecule.

Dalton, like Leucippus and Democritus, thought that atoms were indivisible, but that turns out to be incorrect. As scientists discovered more elements, they began to wonder what distinguished one element from another. Might atoms be made of even smaller particles, just as molecules are made from atoms? By the end of the nineteenth century, physicists (scientists who study matter and energy) had begun to find evidence that the answer was yes.

Today, students like you learn that atoms contain **protons**, **neutrons**, and **electrons**. But that is not the full set of subatomic particles. This series, Exploring the Subatomic World, tells how those particles were discovered and how they combine to give atoms their properties. This book is the story of one of those particles. It will carry you deep inside the atom to explore the nucleus. There you will find neutrons and the forces that act on them. You will also discover how understanding neutrons enabled us to unleash great power, first in war and then for the benefit of the world.

1 ATOMS
and Molecules

The ancient Greek idea of atoms was very different from the one we have today. They suggested that the atoms of each different kind of matter had a shape and texture that matched the properties of the substance itself. They expected that water atoms would be round and smooth, while the atoms in rock would be hard and sharp or gritty.

Unlike Dalton, they never considered testing their atomic theory by observing and experimenting. That was not because atoms were too small to see (although they are). It was because testing ideas through observation, a cornerstone of modern science, had not yet become part of human culture. In fact, Greek philosophy took an opposite approach, valuing pure human thought above all else. Logical thinking and reason alone were considered sufficient to deduce the truth. Great thinkers such as Socrates, Aristotle, and Plato used their powerful minds and logic to deduce what they believed to be the truth about the world around them.

Aristotle was considered so brilliant that people would rarely question his ideas, even long after his death. For nearly two thousand years, people simply accepted Aristotle's explanation that all the world's matter was made of four elements: earth, air, fire, and water. The idea of atoms all but disappeared. Today we know that both Democritus and Aristotle were right in one way but wrong in another.

There is a limit to how small a piece of matter can be cut and still remain the same substance. Leucippus and Democritus were right about that. But since most substances are compounds, the smallest possible piece

is a molecule instead of an atom. Furthermore, that piece is not indivisible. Molecules of compounds can be divided into atoms, which contain even smaller (subatomic) particles.

Aristotle's concept of elements was correct, but not the ones he wrote about. The number of natural elements is nearly one hundred, and Aristotle's four are not among them. Water is a compound of hydrogen and oxygen. Both earth and air are mixtures containing both elements and compounds. Fire is not matter— it is energy produced by a rapid chemical reaction.

Seventeenth-Century Image of Aristotle. This drawing in Thomas Stanley's 1655 book, *The History of Philosophy*, illustrates the high esteem scholars of that period had for Aristotle and his ideas.

The Rise of Chemistry

Between ancient Greek natural philosophy and today's atom-based chemistry came a practice called **alchemy**, in which people tried to make certain substances out of other substances. Most often, alchemists were searching for ways to turn less valuable metals into gold. We now know that the techniques they used—which often produced real chemical changes—were doomed to failure. Both ancient alchemy and modern chemistry can rearrange the way atoms are combined, but they can't change one kind of atom (such as lead) into another (like gold).

An Alchemist at Work. In this circa 1660 engraving based on a painting by David Teniers the Younger, an alchemist is tending a flame as he attempts to turn a less valuable metal into gold.

Many of the most famous alchemists were frauds, but others developed a rudimentary knowledge of matter and techniques that they used to extract or purify many useful elements and compounds from natural minerals and ores. By the beginning of the eighteenth century, alchemy had become chemistry. Chemists of that time investigated many important phenomena in their laboratories including the behavior of gases at different pressures and temperatures, processes of combustion and corrosion, and the relationship between electricity and matter. None of these were fully understood, but the chemists collected a great deal of valuable information through systematic scientific measurement and study.

The turn of the nineteenth century marked a change in John Dalton's life. He had been working in meteorology, but he realized that he could understand the weather better if he knew more about the gases of the air. So he changed his scientific focus to chemistry. It did not take long before he figured out that the old idea of atoms would explain many properties of gases and chemical processes. In 1810, Dalton published *A New System of Chemical Philosophy*, a book that revolutionized his new field.

Dalton's "new system" began with the statement that all matter is made of atoms. He went on to explain that each element is made of a particular kind of atom, that all of its atoms are identical to each other, and that atoms join together to form compounds. This is always in small whole numbers; no fractions allowed. The properties of atoms, such as weight, distinguish one element from another.

Applying those simple rules, he determined the **atomic weight** of different elements. He set the atomic weight of hydrogen, the lightest element, at one unit, and he calculated the atomic weight of other atoms from that. He wasn't always correct, but it was clear he was making progress. For instance, he knew that water had eight times the oxygen as hydrogen by weight. But he mistakenly assumed that a water molecule had one atom of each element, and therefore he concluded that the atomic weight of oxygen was eight. When later research showed that water molecules had two atoms of hydrogen for each oxygen atom, scientists corrected the atomic weight of oxygen to sixteen.

Organizing the Elements

Dalton had given chemistry a new basic vocabulary. Scientists everywhere spoke of elements and compounds, atoms and molecules, and, of course, they asked questions. How many elements are there, they wondered, and how could they classify the growing number?

Several properties provided hints of similarities and patterns among the elements. These included melting or boiling points, densities (how much each cubic centimeter weighs), the way one element combines with others, and the properties of the resulting compounds. Still, no one had successfully turned those hints into a classification scheme—until Russian chemist Dmitri Ivanovich Mendeleyev (1834–1907), a professor at St. Petersburg University, had a flash of insight in 1869.

Mendeleyev was a walking encyclopedia of the sixty-three known elements, with detailed knowledge of their properties. He decided to make a set of cards, one for each element, listing the known properties of each, and arranged them in order of increasing atomic weight. For three days and nights, he would lay the cards on his table, grouping and regrouping them, hoping to discover a classification scheme before leaving on a long-scheduled train trip to the countryside, where his

Dalton's Table of Atomic Symbols. John Dalton produced this table for a lecture at the Manchester Mechanic's Institution on October 19, 1835. It includes symbols for individual elements and shows how they combine to form common compounds of as many as ten atoms. Note that he thought water, listed first among the compounds, had only one hydrogen atom for each oxygen atom.

How Do We Know that Water Is H_2O?

Have you ever heard people call water "good old H-2-O"? That term comes from the chemical formula for water (H_2O), which means it is a molecule formed from two hydrogen atoms and one oxygen atom. Scientists first discovered that and many other chemical formulas in experiments with combining gases.

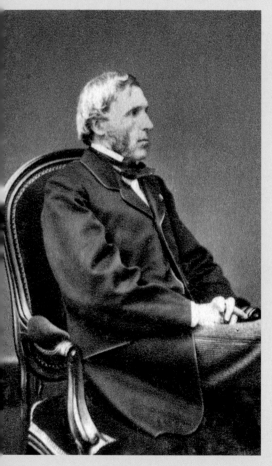

French chemist Joseph Louis Gay-Lussac (1778–1850) was among the first to do so. In 1808, he described what happened when two gases reacted to form another gas. From performing numerous experiments, he found the volumes of the reacting gases at the same temperature and pressure were always in the ratio of simple whole numbers. For instance, when hydrogen burned in oxygen to form water, for every two cubic meters (21.6 cubic feet) of hydrogen burned,

Joseph Louis Gay-Lussac. Gay-Lussac discovered that the volumes of combining gases and their compounds were always in small, whole-number ratios. That principle is now known as Gay-Lussac's Law.

it took one cubic meter (10.8 cu. ft.) of oxygen. The result was two cubic meters (528 gallon) of water vapor. He proposed that discovery as a law of nature.

Italian scientist Amadeo Avogadro (1776–1856) read about Gay-Lussac's proposed law of gases, and he tried to understand why nature behaved that way. He thought about the nature of gases in containers, and he envisioned lots of molecules colliding with each other and with the container walls. Because the molecules were so far apart, it didn't matter what kind of molecules they were. In 1811, he published his conclusion that any gas having the same temperature and pressure and occupying the same volume had the same number of molecules—another law of nature for gases.

Combining the two laws, it became clear that Gay-Lussac's law of whole-number volumes was also a law of whole number of atoms or molecules. Thus a molecule of water had to contain two hydrogen atoms and one oxygen atom. Other experiments showed that hydrogen molecules were two hydrogen atoms combined, or H_2, and, likewise, oxygen molecules were O_2. Therefore Gay-Lussac's experiment showed this reaction.

$$2H_2 + O_2 \longrightarrow 2H_2O$$

(2 hydrogen molecules and 1 oxygen
molecule produce 2 molecules of water)

Dmitri Ivanovich Mendeleyev. Mendeleyev is considered one of the greatest chemists in history for his creation of the periodic table of the elements.

family owned an estate. Just before the time came for him leave, the weary professor fell asleep and dreamed of playing solitaire with his deck of element cards.

Awake on the train, Mendeleyev played element solitaire. By the time he arrived at his destination, an arrangement of elements in rows and columns had begun to take shape. With the elements ordered by increasing atomic weight (down the columns from top to bottom), he discovered that the horizontal rows of elements aligned themselves to match a chemical property known as valence. That property relates to the numbers of atoms of two combining elements. For example, the alkali metals—lithium, sodium, potassium, rubidium, and cesium—which all have a valence of +1, fell into alignment across one row. Likewise, the nonmetals called halogens—

fluorine, chlorine, bromine, and iodine—with a valence of −1, lined up in another row. Because of its repeating pattern, Mendeleyev called this arrangement the **periodic table of the elements**. (Today, the usual arrangement of the periodic table is increasing **atomic masses** across rows, with the valences aligned in columns.)

The table was not perfect—most notably, it had gaps. But those did not bother Mendeleyev, who stated boldly that those would be filled by undiscovered elements. He was right. When those elements were discovered, their atomic weights, densities, and other properties were just as he predicted! But even though he predicted what the atomic weights would be, he had only a pattern but not a principle to explain those values. The full explanation would not come for several decades, because it required the discovery of particles of matter even smaller than an atom—including neutrons.

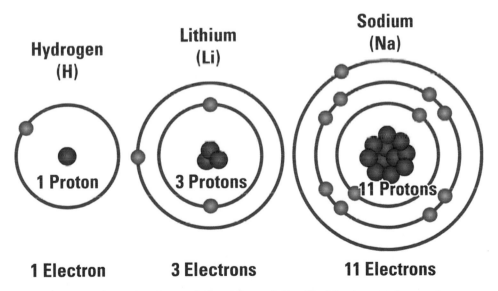

Hydrogen (H)

Lithium (Li)

Sodium (Na)

1 Proton

3 Protons

11 Protons

1 Electron

3 Electrons

11 Electrons

Three Atoms with the Same Valence. In the modern periodic table of the elements, the atoms in the same column have the same valence, a quantity that describes how they form compounds with other atoms. It took scientists more than fifty years and the discovery of subatomic particles to understand the physical basis of valence, which turns out to be related to the number of electrons outside of the atoms' filled inner "shells." Hydrogen, lithium, and sodium, as illustrated here, all have one valence electron.

Some Elements Discovered by 1869

Mendeleyev's periodic table was built on many centuries of discovery. Here, in order of increasing atomic weight, are some of the elements he knew well.

Hydrogen (H): Discovered in 1766 by Henry Cavendish in London, England.

Lithium (Li): Discovered in 1817 by J. A. Arfwedson in Sweden.

Boron (B): Discovered in 1808 by J. L. Gay-Lussac and L. J. Thenard as well as Sir Humphry Davy.

Carbon (C): Discovered in prehistoric times.

Nitrogen (N): Discovered in 1772 by Daniel Rutherford in Edinburgh, Scotland, as well as in the early 1770s by Carl Wilhelm Scheele in Sweden, Henry Cavendish, and Joseph Priestly in England.

Oxygen (O): Discovered independently around 1772 by Carl Wilhelm Scheele in Sweden and 1774 by Joseph Priestley in England.

Aluminum (Al): Discovered in 1825 by Hans Christian Oersted in Denmark.

Calcium (Ca): Discovered in 1808 by Sir Humphry Davy in London, England.

Iron (Fe): Discovered by ancient civilizations.

Zinc (Zn): Known in India and China before 1500 and to the Greeks and Romans before 20 BCE.

History on a Page. Mendeleyev's periodic table in his own handwriting from 1869 listing the elements down the columns in order of increasing atomic weight, and across rows with atoms of the same valence.

2 THE NUCLEUS

T he discovery and success of the periodic table led scientists to new questions, including these: What makes the periodic table periodic? What is responsible for the differences between the elements? The answer begins with this fact: depite the meaning of *atomos*, atoms are not indivisible. Science has revealed that they contain subatomic particles.

The first subatomic particle to be discovered was the electron. J. J. Thomson (1856–1940) of Cambridge University in England was studying an interesting electrical phenomenon in glass tubes from which most of the air had been removed. When scientists inserted pairs of electrodes into the tubes and connected them to the opposite ends of a source of electricity such as a battery, they observed a glow near the negative electrode, or cathode. They didn't know what was causing the light, but they called it a cathode ray. Some scientists thought cathode rays were probably waves of energy; others said they were streams of particles.

In 1897, Thomson demonstrated that cathode rays were streams of the smallest particles ever known. He called them "corpuscles," but today we call them electrons. By his measurements, a single corpuscle had less than a thousandth of the mass of the lightest atom—hydrogen. A more precise measurement later showed that it is even smaller, about $\frac{1}{1800}$ as massive. Yet it had as much negative electrical charge as that atom might carry in positive charge.

Joseph John Thomson in 1900. J. J. Thomson was the first scientist to discover a subatomic particle, the electron, in 1897.

Ernest Rutherford. This picture shows Ernest Rutherford in 1908, the year he won the Nobel Prize in Chemistry for his work with radioactive materials. His greatest discovery lay ahead. In 1909, he and his students Hans Geiger and Ernest Marsden began experiments that led to the discovery of the atomic nucleus two years later.

It wasn't long before Thomson and others recognized that electrons were contained within all atoms. Furthermore, they were involved not only in electrical phenomena but also in the relationships between electricity and chemistry—including valence. Since atoms are electrically neutral, they must contain an amount of positive electricity to balance the negatively charged electrons, and that positive charge had to carry most of the atom's mass. But what was that positively charged subatomic matter, and what was the internal structure of atoms?

J. J. Thomson suggested a model of atoms that resembled a popular British dessert, plum pudding, with tiny electron plums scattered throughout a positively charged bulk. Thomson's plum pudding atoms seemed sensible, but scientific models must be tested, and Ernest Rutherford (1871–1937) created a method: he probed the inside of atoms with radioactive beams.

Rutherford had left his native New Zealand in 1895 to study the recently discovered phenomenon of **radioactivity** at Cambridge in Thomson's Cavendish Laboratory. By the time he left to become a professor at McGill University in Montreal, Canada, in 1898, he had discovered that radiation comes in two distinct forms: in the form of particles or in the form of waves. He named them "**alpha rays**" and "**beta rays**" after the first two letters of the Greek alphabet. At McGill, he and colleague Frederick Soddy (1877–1956) discovered a third form of radioactivity in 1902, which they designated "**gamma rays**." They also discovered that alpha radiation was a stream of energetic positively charged particles, while beta radiation consisted of high-speed negatively charged particles.

In 1907, Rutherford returned to England, becoming a professor at the University of Manchester and bursting with ideas about how to use radioactive beams. He planned to begin by shooting **alpha particles** through thin metallic foils. He realized that observing the way the alpha particles deflected, or scattered, would reveal the arrangement of the atoms in the foil—their size and spacing, perhaps even their shape. He and his student Hans Geiger (1882–1945) developed an instrument to detect and count the alphas. They also demonstrated, as Rutherford had suspected, that alpha particles were helium atoms without their electrons.

By 1909, they were ready to begin alpha-**scattering** experiments. Nearly all the alphas passed straight through the foil or deflected only slightly. That result fit Thomson's model, except for one puzzling result: the counters were very accurate, and a few alpha particles were missing. Rutherford and Geiger had measured alpha scattering in every direction that seemed likely, but now they had to consider unlikely directions far off to the side. Intrigued, but not wanting to divert Geiger from his main task, Rutherford turned to Ernest Marsden (1889–1970), a young student just learning the techniques of research. Marsden found the missing alpha particles. Astonishingly, not only had some alphas scattered far to the left or right of the original detector positions, but a few had even scattered backward.

What did the result mean? Rutherford realized that the atom was very different than anyone had imagined up to that

Rutherford's Lucky Break

Rutherford was a brilliant student and researcher, but he almost missed his chance to study and work with J. J. Thomson. In New Zealand, he had been studying how radio waves—then called Hertzian waves after German physicist Heinrich Hertz (1857–94), who first produced them—interacted with small magnetized needles. That led him to develop one of the first radio receivers, a major invention in the fast-growing field of telegraphy.

That success made him a strong candidate to receive a major research scholarship to study in England in 1895. Unfortunately, the scholarship committee ranked him second, behind a chemist. Since only one scholarship was awarded, it was offered to that chemist. Fortunately for Rutherford, that chemist had recently married and decided to stay in New Zealand. Rutherford was next in line, and he eagerly accepted the prize. His choice was Cambridge University's Cavendish Laboratory, and the rest is history.

point. In 1911, he explained his results with a new atomic model. He envisioned atoms as miniature solar systems held together by the electric force instead of gravity. (Opposite electric charges attract each other.) He called the positively charged central body the **nucleus**. Rutherford noted that his results showed that the positive charge was concentrated in a region about $\frac{1}{10,000}$ of the size of the whole atom. The rest of the atom was empty space, except for the lightweight electrons, which he visualized as being like planets in orbit around that minuscule but massive nuclear sun.

That structure explained why most alpha particles would pass through the foil with little scattering: They rarely came close enough to a nucleus to be deflected very much. Only on those rare occasions when a fast-moving alpha particle made a nearly direct hit on a much heavier nucleus would it scatter, and then it would be jolted so much that a sideways or even backward deflection would be possible.

Overweight Nuclei

The nuclear model of atoms was quickly accepted, but that immediately raised new questions. For example, what was in the nucleus? Rutherford performed more experiments with alpha particles. He also became convinced that the hydrogen nucleus was a basic subatomic particle. He first called those nuclei "H particles" but renamed them protons in 1917 when he detected them following alpha bombardment of boron, fluorine, sodium, aluminum, phosphorus, and nitrogen.

That discovery changed scientific thinking about the meaning of **atomic number**, which was at first defined as the number of an atom's electrons. Since it was not difficult to turn most atoms into ions by adding or taking away an

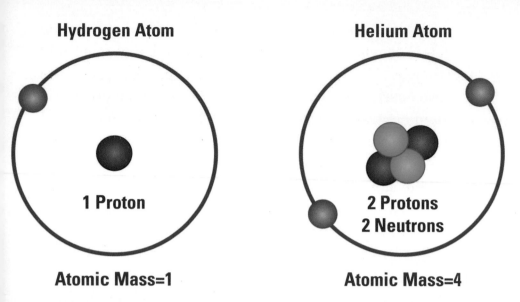

Hydrogen Atom

1 Proton

Atomic Mass=1

Helium Atom

2 Protons
2 Neutrons

Atomic Mass=4

Extra Mass. Once Rutherford discovered the atomic nucleus, he ran into a different problem. The mass of larger nuclei grew faster than their electrical charge. For example, helium nuclei had twice the charge but four times the mass of hydrogen nuclei. Rutherford proposed that nuclei were made up of positively charged protons plus neutral particles of approximately the same mass as protons (later called neutrons), leading to the model shown here.

electron or two, atomic number was redefined as the total positive charge in the nucleus. Hydrogen, the simplest atom with atomic number one, has a nucleus with a single proton. Helium, with atomic number two, has two protons, and so forth. But things are not quite that simple when atomic weight— or atomic mass, the term physicists prefer—is added to the picture.

The atomic mass of hydrogen is one, and the hydrogen nucleus has one proton. But the helium nucleus (the alpha particle), which has two protons, carries an atomic mass of four. The discrepancy gets worse as atomic numbers increase. For atomic number 82 (lead) the atomic mass is approximately 207. (The atomic masses turn out not to be exact whole numbers, and that will be explained later.) Protons do not account for even half the mass of most nuclei. Are there more protons, or might other subatomic particles exist?

A Problem With
the Planetary Model

The planetary model explained the results of Rutherford's scattering experiments, yet it had one serious problem that came from the motion of the electrons. Whenever an electrically charged object is changing its velocity, either by changes in speed or direction of motion, the equations of electricity and magnetism state that it must radiate electromagnetic waves (such as light or radio waves), which carry energy. Orbiting electrons are always changing direction, which means that they should constantly lose energy. That would cause them to spiral inward toward the nucleus. But if that actually happened, every atom in the universe would have collapsed long ago.

Nature's electromagnetic laws guided the orbits of electrons in atoms. Yet the same laws did not seem to be operating when it came to radiating energy when those electrons changed direction. Rutherford recognized the problem, but could not fully explain it. He could only guess that something was special about electrons in atoms. The planetary model of the atom was clearly imperfect or incomplete. Still, it was an excellent start to discovering the subatomic world.

Rutherford believed that the extra mass led to a different, and very important, question about nuclei: What held them together so tightly? Electrical force increases very rapidly as the separation of charged bodies decreases. Cutting the separation in half multiplies the force by four (two times two). At one-third the separation, the force is nine times as great (three times

Carbon (C⁶)

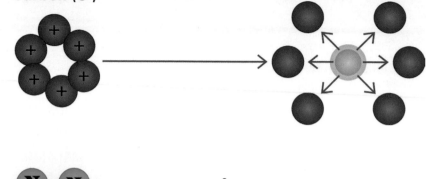

Electrical repulsion
of protons would
destroy the nucleus.

Carbon (C$_{12}^{6}$)

Neutrons and protons
are bound by the strong
nuclear force.

Holding the Nucleus Together. Rutherford thought his neutral particles did more than solve the mass problem. They might also serve as the glue to hold the protons of a nucleus together even though they repel each other electrically.

three). Since the nucleus is about $\frac{1}{10,000}$ the size of an atom, and since two positive or two negative electric charges repel each other, two protons in the nucleus would push apart with a force millions of times as great as the attractive force between a proton and an orbiting electron. Such powerful forces would surely blow the nucleus apart—unless there was a stronger force within the nucleus to hold it together.

Rutherford realized that whatever gives the nucleus more mass is probably also responsible for holding it together. That led to his next important subatomic idea, the neutron, and to the discovery of two previously unknown forces within the nucleus.

3 NUCLEAR
Forces

Before Rutherford discovered the nucleus he was already famous. He won the 1908 Nobel Prize in Chemistry for his studies of radioactivity. He was responsible for discovering alpha and beta radiation and, with Frederick Soddy, gamma rays. They and other scientists soon learned how to identify each radioactive element by the energy of its alpha, beta, and gamma rays. Remarkably, radioactive decay achieved the kind of changes that alchemists had sought— transforming one element into another—a process that came to be called **transmutation**.

Rutherford and Soddy were particularly interested in tracking the elements from their original form to their new forms. Since they had not yet discovered the nucleus, they did not yet know that the chemical changes they were observing were the result of nuclear events. But they could describe the changes in terms of atomic mass and atomic number. For instance, when an atom emits an alpha particle, its atomic mass decreases by four units and its atomic number decreases by two. Likewise, the emission of a **beta particle** increases the atomic number by one unit but doesn't change atomic mass.

Both emissions result in the transmutation of an atom of a "parent" element into an atom of a different element, the "daughter." The new atom is frequently more radioactive than its predecessor, so there is a chain of alpha or beta decays from one atom to another to another, and so on. A gamma ray is pure energy, with neither mass nor electric charge, so the emission of a gamma does not cause transmutation. However, a radioactive atom emits a gamma ray only following an alpha or beta emission, so a gamma is a sign that transmutation has recently occurred.

Rutherford and Soddy studied different radioactive decay chains. They discovered in some cases that the daughter atoms in different chains behaved the same way chemically, which meant that they were the same elements. Yet they found that the two chemicals had different atomic masses. Soddy called such atoms with the same chemical behavior but different atomic masses "isotopes," and he quickly realized that many nonradioactive atoms also had more than one isotopic form

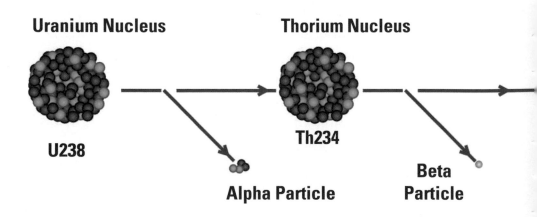

Uranium Nucleus

Thorium Nucleus

U238

Th234

Alpha Particle

Beta Particle

as well. To distinguish one isotope from another, scientists began denoting atoms by their chemical symbol and their atomic mass. For instance, natural chlorine is a mixture of two isotopes, Cl^{35} and the less common Cl^{37}, with an average atomic mass of 35.47.

The Search for the Neutron

By 1920, the year after Rutherford had replaced the retiring J. J. Thomson as leader of the Cavendish Laboratory at Cambridge University, no one questioned that the hydrogen nucleus was a single proton or that alpha particles were helium nuclei with two protons and an atomic mass of four units. The mass that didn't come from protons remained a puzzle.

Some scientists suggested it was due to extra protons plus an equal number of electrons. Rutherford disagreed. His argument was that the nucleus "is so small that any electron inside it would experience a powerful electrical attraction to any proton, and the pair would immediately bind together." The result would be an electrically neutral subatomic particle

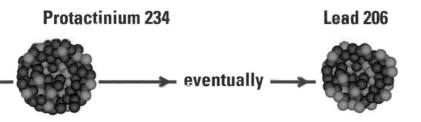

Protactinium 234   **Lead 206**

eventually

A Radioactive Series. Rutherford and Soddy discovered that one radioactive decay was often followed by another until the sequence led to a stable isotope. Although the atomic nucleus was not understood, this diagram shows their discovery of the sequence of nuclear changes that takes place over billions of years, transforming a uranium-238 nucleus to lead-206.

Beta Rays and Neutrinos

Rutherford's explanation of beta rays was flawed. When he stated that beta particles came from the transformation of a neutron within the nucleus into a proton and an electron, he left out one very important piece of the puzzle.

When the nucleus of a particular radioactive isotope nucleus emits an alpha particle, that alpha always carries the same exact amount of energy. That allows scientists to identify the isotope by the energy of its alpha particle. The same is true of gamma rays. But beta rays are different. They can have any amount of energy from nearly zero up to a certain maximum.

That caused a problem, because the scientific principle of conservation of energy was never violated in any other circumstance. Energy could change form, but it was never gained or lost. The famous equation $E = mc^2$ showed that mass was a form of energy. When a neutron transforms into a proton and an electron, the nucleus loses a small amount of mass that transforms into energy. The proton stays in place, but the electron leaves the nucleus as a beta particle and carries some of that energy with it.

Experiments showed that the energy the beta particle carried was never more than the lost mass. But it could be much less. To conserve energy, Wolfgang Pauli (1900–1958) proposed in 1930 that another particle was also emitted. That particle could not carry electric charge or have much mass, which makes it very hard to detect. He called it the neutrino, for "little neutral one." The neutrino was a central part of a theory of beta decay published by Enrico Fermi (1901–1954) in 1933, and it was finally detected in 1956.

Enrico Fermi. One of the greatest physicists of the mid-twentieth century, Fermi developed a theory of beta decay that included the emission of a very light, electrically neutral particle, which he called the neutrino, meaning little neutral one in his native Italian.

he called a neutron. Alpha particles, for example, consisted of two protons, each with one unit of positive electric charge, and two uncharged neutrons.

Rutherford now explained that alpha radiation occurs when two protons and two neutrons come together within a large unstable nucleus and burst free. Likewise, he claimed that beta emission results from the splitting of a neutron in an unstable nucleus, further resulting in a proton and an electron. Since electrons are so light, the new nucleus would have approximately the same atomic mass, but the added proton would increase its atomic number by one. Rutherford was right about alpha emission and almost right about beta emission. Later research showed that every beta particle has a tiny partner, a subatomic sprite called a neutrino with no electric charge and so little mass that no one has succeeded in measuring it.

Of course, Rutherford knew that any theory, no matter how good, still required proof. So he set out to find neutrons, and that was no easy task. During the 1920s, a number of scientists developed instruments that enabled them to see the paths of subatomic particles. These devices depended on the interactions between the subatomic particles and matter, especially their ability to ionize gases that they passed through. That worked fine for charged particles such as protons and alphas, but not neutrons.

Finally in 1932, James Chadwick (1891–1974), one of Rutherford's colleagues at the Cavendish Laboratory, discovered a way to detect neutrons indirectly but convincingly. In 1930, German researcher Walther Bothe (1891–1957) and his student Herbert Becker discovered that when a beam of particles bombarded beryllium metal, which had four protons and five neutrons in the nuclei of its naturally occurring isotope Be^9,

Electron ●

Neutron
about to decay

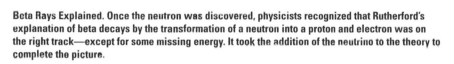

Proton

Neutrino ●

Beta Rays Explained. Once the neutron was discovered, physicists recognized that Rutherford's explanation of beta decays by the transformation of a neutron into a proton and electron was on the right track—except for some missing energy. It took the addition of the neutrino to the theory to complete the picture.

the result was a powerful beam of neutral radiation. They assumed these beams were gamma rays because of the ease with which they penetrated matter.

Irene Curie (1897–1956), the daughter of the famous Pierre and Marie Curie, and her husband Frederic Joliot (1900–1958), later discovered that the neutral radiation would knock protons out of paraffin wax, which is rich in hydrogen. That was a surprising result for gamma rays, which could knock light electrons loose but had never been observed to eject heavier particles such as protons. When Chadwick heard of that result, he knew right away that the neutral beam had to be composed of neutrons.

Chadwick performed a series of experiments in which he allowed the beam to collide with a variety of gases. By measuring the scattering of the nuclei of those gas atoms, he was able to measure the mass of the particles in the beam, which turned out to be almost exactly the same mass as a proton, just as Rutherford had predicted for neutrons. That result established the basic atomic structure we now know: A tiny but massive nucleus of positively charged protons and electrically neutral neutrons, occupying only about a ten-thousandth of the atom's diameter, surrounded by light electrons in equal number to the protons.

Neutrons and Nuclear Forces

At the time Rutherford was probing the atomic nucleus, two other revolutions in physics were also underway: **quantum mechanics** and relativity. Albert Einstein (1879–1955) had a hand in both. You have probably heard about Einstein's famous equation $E = mc^2$. This equation comes from his 1905 work on the **theory of relativity** and expresses the unexpected idea that mass (m) and energy (E) are two aspects of the same property of a physical system. Since they are measured in different units, we need a conversion factor to match them up, just as you might change a measurement in inches to centimeters by multiplying by 2.54. To convert mass to energy, you multiply by the speed of light (c) times itself (or squared).

The power of that simple equation shows up in radioactive decay. When a radioactive nucleus emits an alpha particle,

Albert Einstein in 1919. This colorized photo shows the great physicist Albert Einstein at the height of his career. In 1905, he changed the way physicists viewed space and time, matter and energy, and the meaning of the speed of light with his special theory of relativity. That same year, his explanation of the photoelectric effect launched the quantum revolution.

you might expect sum of the mass of the alpha particle and the mass of the daughter nucleus to add up to mass of the parent nucleus. But that is not true. The total mass after the decay is less than the original mass. The missing mass, when converted to energy by Einstein's famous equation, is exactly the amount of energy carried by the alpha particle.

Einstein solved another puzzle in 1905. The puzzle concerned the photoelectric effect, in which light could

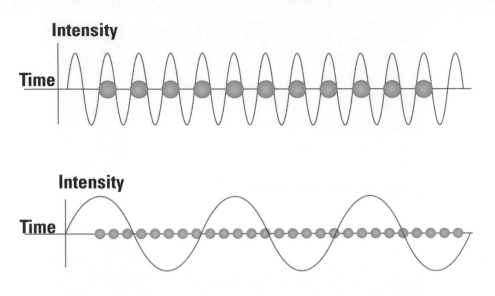

Trick or Treat? Planck considered his idea of light quanta—packets that contained an amount of energy equal to a constant multiplied by the frequency of the waves—to be nothing more than a mathematical trick. But Einstein's analysis of the photoelectric effect showed that they were real. A single high-frequency light quantum from the dimmest light source had enough energy to knock an electron loose from a metal, but low frequency quanta from the brightest sources produced no electric current.

knock electrons free from metals—but only if its color was far enough toward the ultraviolet end of the **spectrum**. The color of the light was a measure of the frequency of light waves. That frequency had to reach a threshold before the light freed electrons.

Einstein recognized a similarity between that threshold and an odd idea developed a few years earlier by Max Planck (1858–1947) in his calculations of the spectrum produced by a hot body. Planck's equation depended on having light energy coming not in smooth waves like water, but in a stream of packets called quanta (singular, quantum). In that equation, the energy of a quantum was equal to a constant times the frequency of the light wave. That constant came to be called Planck's constant.

Planck didn't believe that quanta actually existed, but they made his calculations work. Einstein's breakthrough was to recognize that the photoelectric effect was evidence that light quanta, which eventually came to be called **photons**, were real.

That was the beginning of a new field called quantum mechanics, which states that all subatomic particles are quanta, and, just like photons, they act like waves under certain circumstances and particles at other times. For example, electrons in atoms have certain wavelike states that are allowed, each corresponding to a certain energy level specified by four quantum numbers. The quantum numbers create a pattern as atoms increase in atomic number. Certain numbers of electrons act as filled "shells," while the remaining electrons are available for atoms to interact. The pattern is the same one discovered by Mendeleyev. The table of elements is periodic because of quantum mechanics.

Quantum mechanics has been a spectacularly successful theory. It has changed the way physicists look at the basic forces of nature. Applying the laws of **electromagnetism** at the atomic level required a new mathematical approach called quantum electrodynamics, in which attraction and repulsion are the result of an interchange of photons between electrically charged quanta, such as electrons and protons— and that takes us back into the nucleus. Since protons repel one another by exchanging photons, what keeps the nucleus from blowing itself apart? Another force must act inside the nucleus, and it must have something to do with neutrons.

That force is called the strong nuclear force, or simply the strong force. (Another nuclear force is called the weak force, and it explains beta decay.) The strong force has unusual properties compared to electromagnetism. For example, despite its power within the nucleus, the strong force must have a short range, quickly becoming weaker than electromagnetic

Quantum Mechanics and Orbiting Electrons

Quantum Mechanics solved the problem of orbiting electrons in Rutherford's model of the atom. Danish physicist Neils Bohr (1885–1962) took the first steps when he described a set of special electron orbits could exist without radiating electromagnetic waves. For those orbits, a physical quantity called the electron's angular momentum had to be equal to a whole number times Planck's constant. Bohr didn't have an explanation for why those orbits were special, but they successfully predicted the spectrum of light produced when electricity made hydrogen gas glow.

Once the idea of wavelike properties of electrons came into being, it turned out that the circumference of each of Bohr's allowed orbits was equal to a whole number of electron wavelengths. That is what made them special. Instead of orbiting, those electrons were like the standing waves of a violin string (which produces a fundamental tone and certain overtones, but no notes in between). Since the electron waves didn't rotate, they could obey the laws of electromagnetism without radiating energy away. Rutherford's problem had disappeared.

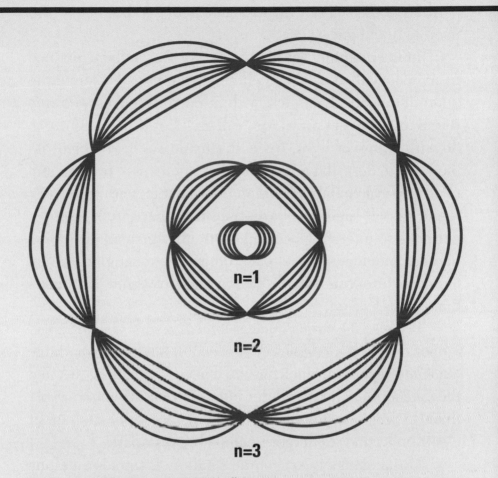

Electron Waves. In quantum mechanics, just as light waves can have particle-like properties, particles can have wavelike behavior. This drawing shows the three lowest energy levels of an electron in an atom. In the lowest level, the circumference of the orbit is one electron wavelength. The second level has a circumference of two electron wavelengths, and so on for higher energies.

forces as you move away from the nucleus. Otherwise, nuclei of different atoms would be drawn together and the universe would be one giant atom. Yet within the nucleus, there must be a limit to the power of the strong force when particles get too close. Otherwise, nuclear matter would crush itself to nothingness.

In the quantum world, nuclear forces can be explained by a theory called quantum chromodynamics. It is similar to quantum electrodynamics, with a few differences. *Chromo* refers to the Greek word for "**color**," but it has nothing to do with colors of light. Instead, physicists have borrowed the word to describe a property that nucleons—protons and neutrons—have through which they interact with the strong force, just as electric charge is the property that enables particles to interact electromagnetically. Instead of trading photons, nucleons attract each other by exchanging quanta called **pi mesons**, which have a mass of about 250 times that of an electron.

Because the strong nuclear force has such a short range, it does not always completely succeed in holding a very large nucleus together. Its nucleons are constantly rearranging, and they sometimes form smaller clusters that are more stable than the large nucleus itself. The clusters repel each other electrically, and the larger nucleus breaks apart.

Most commonly, one of the smaller clusters is an alpha particle, and the result is a familiar form of radioactivity. But in some large nuclei, the clusters are both medium sized nuclei, and the result is a process called nuclear fission that blows the nucleus to pieces and releases lots of energy. Remarkably, people have figured out ways to harness that fission energy. How that happens and what can be done with the energy is the main topic of this book's final chapter.

4 NEUTRONS
and Nuclear Fission

What causes radioactivity? For about a quarter-century after radioactivity was discovered, its cause was not understood. Rutherford and others learned a lot about alpha, beta, and gamma rays, but they did not understand the physical principles that cause it. That is because they hadn't yet discovered the quantum nature of matter and energy.

In the quantum world, nothing stands still. A nucleus is made up of nucleons (protons and neutrons) that are constantly rearranging themselves. Like electrons in atoms, protons and neutrons have states within the nucleus described by quantum numbers. Also like electrons in atoms, those nuclear states have certain closed shells that are particularly stable. For instance, an alpha particle has two protons and two neutrons filling the lowest energy shells for each particle. If four such nucleons in a nucleus join as an alpha particle, it may break loose from the rest of the nucleus. That happens more readily

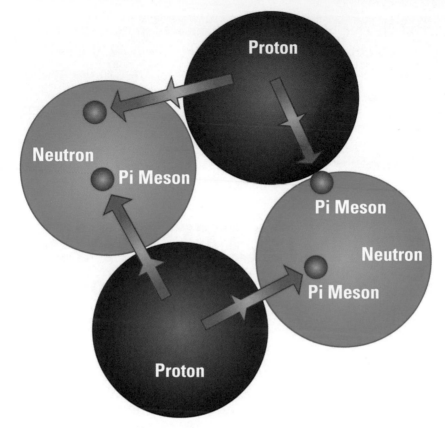

Trading Pions. A nucleus, such as this alpha particle, holds together because of a strong attractive nuclear force between nucleons, which overcomes the powerful electrical repulsion between the protons. The strong force results from the exchange of virtual pions, particles that flicker in and out of existence according to a quantum mechanical rule called the uncertainty principle.

as the nucleus gets so large that the strong force begins to drop off at its outermost parts.

Beta radiation is a similar phenomenon involving the weak force. A free neutron outside a nucleus is unstable because it has more mass than a proton, electron, and neutrino combined. It is always on the verge of blowing itself apart into those particles (this happens in beta decay) except for the weak nuclear force that holds it together. If you could watch such a neutron for about fifteen minutes, it would have a fifty-fifty chance of decaying. Inside most nuclei, the neutrons stay together because of quantum chromodynamic effects. The protons and neutrons are always passing pi mesons back and forth and changing from one type of nucleon to the other. As a result the neutrons don't have enough time to decay.

Those pi mesons are called virtual particles because they have much more mass than that given up by the protons and neutrons that release them. They thus use energy that should not be available. But a rule of quantum mechanics called the uncertainty principle allows them to flicker in and out of existence long enough to travel the short distance between the nucleons. That also explains the short range of the nuclear force, since the virtual particles that carry it disappear too fast for it to have a long range. In larger radioactive nuclei, neutrons stay neutrons a little longer. Sometimes that is long enough that the weak force is not enough to prevent beta decay.

Fission: When Nuclei Split

Besides alpha, beta, and gamma rays, there is one more type of radioactivity that happens when large nuclei spontaneously split apart. It is called nuclear fission.

In 1938, two German physicists, Austrian-born Lise Meitner (1878–1968) and Otto Hahn (1879–1968), began investigating artificial elements beyond uranium (atomic number 92) in the periodic table. Italian physicist Enrico Fermi had first noticed these in 1935 during experiments in which he bombarded uranium with neutrons. A uranium nucleus (U^{238}) would capture a neutron and quickly emit a beta, leaving behind a proton in the new nucleus with atomic number 93 and atomic mass 239 (neptunium 239). The unstable Np^{239} nucleus would emit another beta, leaving behind a nucleus with atomic number 94 and atomic mass 239, plutonium (Pu^{239}).

Long-Term Colleagues. In the early years of the twentieth century, women were a rarity in science. This picture shows Lise Meitner with Otto Hahn in 1913 in a laboratory of the Kaiser Wilhelm Institute in Berlin, Germany. Their collaboration continued until Nazi persecution forced Meitner to flee in 1938, just as they were discovering nuclear fission.

Meitner, Hahn, and the Names of Elements

The story of the relationship between Lise Meitner and Otto Hahn touches on two important historical themes of the first half of the twentieth century: women in science, and the Nazi persecution of Jews and other people whom the Nazis considered to be of a lesser race or lesser character. Meitner was born Jewish but converted to Christianity for convenience. But to the Nazi regime, she was still a Jew.

When Hahn and Meitner began working together in 1902, the director of the Berlin Chemistry Institute did not allow women inside because he thought their hairstyles were fire hazards. Hahn persuaded him to convert a carpenter's shop with an outside entrance into a workplace for her. Yet Hahn never corrected colleagues who addressed him and ignored her. Still, their work and their friendship flourished to the point that Hahn sold a family heirloom to provide Meitner the funds to bribe a border guard to escape the Nazis. After the discovery of fission, when the Nobel Committee honored Hahn, but not Meitner, with the 1944 chemistry prize for the work, Hahn spoke as if it was his alone.

If Meitner felt slighted, she kept her peace about it. She died long before the scientific world corrected the oversight. In 1997, the International Union for Pure and Applied Chemistry gave official names to some artificially created elements. Element 109 was named Meitnerium in her honor. Element 105, unofficially known as Hahnium until that date, was renamed Dubnium to honor the city of Dubna, where it was first produced.

At the same time in Paris, Irene Joliot-Curie and Pavle Savić (1909–1994) had noticed the odd presence in the bombarded uranium of an element that behaved chemically like the much lighter lanthanum (atomic number 57). About to flee Germany for Sweden because of the danger to Jews from the Nazi government, Meitner discussed the odd results with both Hahn and Fritz Strassman (1902–1980), who then tried experiments similar to those of Joliot-Curie and Savić. They found barium (atomic number 56). It was as if uranium nuclei were splitting into two parts.

In Sweden, Meitner enjoyed a year-end visit from her nephew Otto Frisch (1904–1979), also a physicist. They discussed the odd results and figured out what was happening. A large nucleus might behave like a water droplet bouncing back and forth into an elongated hourglass shape and back again. By chance, the distribution of protons and neutrons between the two parts might be just right to form two separate smaller nuclei within the larger one. The electrical force between the two pieces would blast them apart in a process called nuclear fission. Furthermore, because larger nuclei tended to have a larger proportion of neutrons than smaller nuclei, there would be a few neutrons left over. Fission would be even more likely if the nucleus was in an excited state, meaning any quantum state of the system that has a higher energy than the ground state.

Chain Reactions

It didn't take long for scientists all over the world to figure out what might be possible. Each fission event produces some energy and releases several neutrons. If those outgoing neutrons could cause other fissions, the entire piece of matter

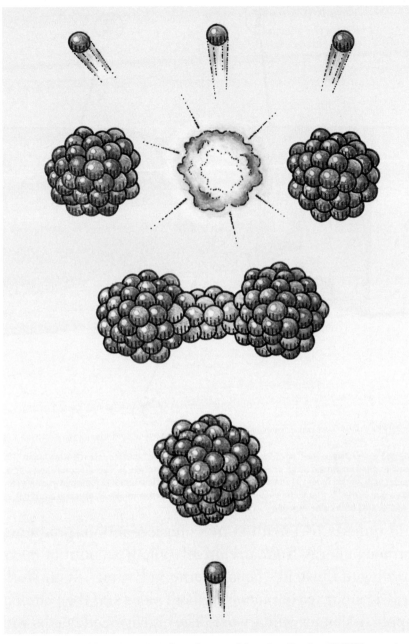

Nuclear Fission and Chain Reactions. Some large nuclei, such as Uranium-235 (U^{235}), occasionally split into two smaller nuclei with several neutrons left over. That process is called spontaneous fission, and scientists describe isotopes that undergo it as fissionable. Fission is much more likely when a nucleus experiences a collision, as shown here. A neutron strikes a nucleus, creating an unstable larger nucleus that promptly undergoes fission. If one or more of the neutrons produced by that fission strike another fissionable nucleus, another fission follows. If enough fissionable nuclei are present, a chain reaction can occur, releasing a large amount of energy in a short time.

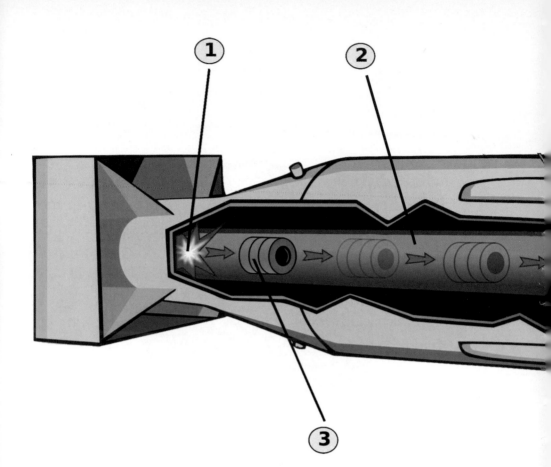

A Nuclear Fission Bomb. The United States was the first nation to build a nuclear fission bomb, commonly called an atomic bomb or A-bomb. It was to end World War II. This diagram shows how one such bomb works. A conventional explosive (1) sends a hollow bullet of enriched uranium (3) through a gun barrel (2). The bullet engulfs a cylinder of enriched uranium (4), creating a critical mass and setting off a chain reaction.

could quickly be engulfed in a chain reaction, producing enormous energy from a relatively small amount of mass, according to Einstein's famous formula $E = mc^2$. With World War II looming, governments on both sides saw the potential to apply fission for military use. They envisioned bombs with frightful power, and they quickly set to work.

Constructing a uranium bomb is not as easy as it might seem. It's easy for neutrons to escape without causing fission in other nuclei. If the average fission event produces three neutrons, then a chain reaction would occur only if at least one-third of the neutrons cause another fission. One problem is that most uranium nuclei are U^{238}, which can capture neutrons but do not decay by fission. Less than one percent of uranium exists as the "fissile" U^{235}.

To make a uranium bomb, the first step is to enrich the uranium, increasing the fraction of U^{235} atoms. An explosion requires at least a certain amount of uranium known as critical mass. With less, most fission neutrons escape without encountering other U^{235} nuclei. Furthermore, that critical mass must be brought together quickly and stay together after igniting the explosion.

The remaining depleted uranium can be used to make bombs in another way. As Fermi had observed, U^{238} can capture a neutron and, after two beta decays, become Pu^{239}, which turns out to be more fissile than U^{235}. The United States ended World War II in 1945 when it used two fission bombs in Japan—the first bomb used uranium and the second used plutonium.

After the war ended, many engineers turned their efforts to building electrical power plants that get their energy from nuclear fission. But they needed to find a design that would control the chain reaction and automatically shut it down in case of trouble. The key to their designs was the fact that most neutrons produced in fission reactions move so fast that they zip out of the material.

Those neutrons would be much more likely to cause a fission reaction if they pass a nucleus slowly enough for it to divert them from their path. So nuclear reactors were built with cores of fuel rods separated by a type of

Controversy Over Fukushima

When a fission reactor fails, it does not release energy like a bomb. The chain reaction stops, but one major concern remains: Will the failure release radioactive material into the environment? Can reactors be designed to keep people safe even when they fail? The failure of three reactors at Japan's Fukushima Dai'ichi plant in 2011 has led to political controversy over those questions.

At Fukushima, a massive earthquake and tsunami disabled the cooling systems that keep the cores of three operating reactors from melting. Even without a chain reaction, the natural radioactivity

in the fuel can create enough heat to melt the fuel rods. Without cooling, the zirconium metal that enclosed those rods became hot enough to react chemically with water and began releasing explosive hydrogen gas. Explosions soon shook the containment buildings and released some radioactivity into the air.

The bigger concern, however, was keeping radioactivity from the melted fuel rods out of the environment. Fortunately, heroic engineers and workers were able keep the worst environmental damage confined to the power plant region itself. Still, full cleanup will take about forty years.

Looking back at the Fukushima events, experts concluded that with better regulation, the reactors would not have failed. Still, all around the world, countries reevaluated their plans to build nuclear reactors. Some, such as Germany, said "No more." Others, such as China, continued with their plans. It will take decades before the world will know which decision was the right one.

Testing for Radioactivity. On February 28, 2012, nearly a year after the triple meltdown at Japan's Fukushima Dai'ichi power plant, a journalist measures radiation levels while covering the cleanup efforts. Because nuclear power provides a significant portion of Japan's energy, its future remains an important political issue.

moderator (water in most cases, but some use graphite) that slows the neutrons enough to cause fission. They also have control rods with materials that absorb neutrons and stop a chain reaction. These must be withdrawn from the core against powerful springs in order to start the chain reaction. In an emergency, or if a spring fails, the control rod snaps into the core and stops the reaction.

Although nuclear power plants generally have excellent safety records, some notable accidents make people fearful about building more. (For an example, see "Controversy Over Fukushima" in this chapter.) Yet the world is facing a crisis every bit as serious as World War II, and nuclear fission once again has the potential of helping to solve it. Our use of fossil fuels to generate electricity is increasing the carbon dioxide (CO_2) content of our atmosphere. Carbon dioxide is called a **greenhouse gas** because it traps heat from Earth's surface that would normally go out into space. Without CO_2, Earth would be cooler by about 50 degrees Fahrenheit.

A Bikini Bombshell. After World War II ended, the United States continued to develop fission bombs. That required test explosions. This picture shows the first of a series of twenty-three tests that began in 1946 and continued through 1958 on Bikini Atoll, a ring of small islands in the Marshall Island chain in the Pacific Ocean. Also in 1946, a French designer of women's swimsuits capitalized on the news of the tests by naming his new creation the bikini. He hoped that its style would create an "explosive commercial and cultural reaction" as powerful as the one produced by mushroom clouds such as this one.

Electricity from Nuclear Energy. Nuclear fission energy now generates electrical power around the world. This power plant is in Temelin, Czech Republic.

But too much CO_2 will lead to global warming, which will cause more extreme storms, heat waves, floods, wildfires, and damage to coastal cities from rising sea level.

So this book ends with a question: Since nuclear power produces no CO_2, nuclear fission may be the best way to solve the problem of global warming. Do you think it is worth the risk?

Glossary

alchemy A predecessor field to chemistry through which
    many people hoped to transform less valuable metals
    into gold but never succeeded.

alpha particle or **alpha ray** A helium nucleus that is emitted
    from some radioactive elements.

atom The smallest bit of matter than can be identified as a
    certain chemical element.

atomic mass or **atomic weight** The mass of a particular
    atom compared to a standard which sets the
    mass of a carbon-12 atom to be exactly 12. For
    a particular isotope, that value is approximately
    the number of protons plus the number of
    neutrons in its nucleus. For a naturally occurring
    element, that value is approximately the number
    of protons plus the average number of neutrons
    in the nuclei of naturally occurring isotopes.

atomic number The number of protons in the nucleus of
    an atom, which determines its chemical identity as
    an element.

beta particle or **beta ray** An electron that is emitted from
    some radioactive elements.

color In the theory of the strong nuclear force, this term is used to refer to the property that particles have that makes them respond to the force, just as electric charge is a property of particles that makes them respond to electromagnetic forces.

electromagnetism A fundamental force of nature, or property of matter and energy, that includes electricity, magnetism, and electromagnetic waves, such as light.

electron A very light subatomic particle (the first to be discovered) that carries negative charge and is responsible for chemical properties of matter.

gamma ray A high-energy photon that is emitted from some radioactive elements.

greenhouse gas A gas that keeps the heat of Earth's surface from escaping into space.

molecule The smallest bit of matter that can be identified as a certain chemical compound.

neutron A subatomic particle with neutral electric charge found in the nucleus of atoms.

nucleus The very tiny, positively charged central part of an atom that carries most of its mass.

periodic table of the elements An arrangement of the elements in rows and columns by increasing atomic number, first proposed by Dmitri Mendeleyev, in which elements in the same column have similar chemical properties.

photon A particle that carries electromagnetic energy, such as light energy.

pi meson A particle that is interchanged by nucleons protons and electrons to produce the strong nuclear force.

proton A subatomic particle with positive electric charge found in the nucleus of atoms.

quantum mechanics A field of physics developed to describe the relationships between matter and energy that accounts for the dual wave-particle nature of both.

radioactivity A property of unstable atoms that causes them to emit alpha, beta, or gamma rays or to undergo fission.

scattering An experimental technique used to detect the shape or properties of an unseen object by observing how other objects deflect from it.

spectrum The mixture of colors contained within a beam of light, or the band produced when those colors are spread out by a prism or other device that separates the colors from each other.

theory of relativity A theory developed by Albert Einstein that deals with the relationship between space and time. Its most famous equation $E = mc^2$ describes the relationship between mass and energy.

transmutation The transformation of a nucleus of one element into another by radioactive emission.

For Further Information

Books

Bortz, Fred. *Meltdown! The Nuclear Disaster in Japan and Our Energy Future*. Minneapolis, MN: Twenty-First Century Books, 2012.

Bortz, Fred. *The Periodic Table of Elements and Dmitry Mendeleyev*. New York: Rosen, 2014.

Bortz, Fred. *Physics: Decade by Decade. Twentieth-Century Science*. New York: Facts On File, 2007.

Challoner, Jack. *The Elements: The New Guide to the Building Blocks of Our Universe*. London: Carlton Books, 2012.

Green, Dan, and Simon Basher. *Extreme Physics*. New York: Kingfisher, 2013.

Hagler, Gina. *Discovering Quantum Mechanics*. New York: Rosen, 2015.

Hollar, Sherman. *Electronics*. New York: Britannica Educational Services, 2012.

Indovina, Shaina Carmel. *Women in Physics*. Broomall, PA: Mason Crest, 2014.

Marsico, Katie. *Key Discoveries in Physical Science*. Minneapolis: Lerner Publications, 2015.

Morgan, Sally. *From Greek Atoms to Quarks: Discovering Atoms*. New York: Heinemann Publishing, 2008.

Websites

American Institute of Physics Center for the History of Physics
www.aip.org/history-programs/physics-history

This site includes several valuable online exhibits from the history of physics, including The Discovery of the Electron and Rutherford's Nuclear World.

The Nobel Foundation Prizes for Physics
www.nobelprize.org/nobel_prizes/physics

Read about past Nobel Prize winners, including J. J. Thomson, Ernest Rutherford, Louis de Broglie, Albert Einstein, George Paget Thomson, Richard Feynman, Enric Fermi, and others. Each entry includes quick biographical facts and brief summaries of their award-winning contributions to physics.

The Science Museum (U.K.)
www.sciencemuseum.org.uk

This site includes the online exhibit Atomic Firsts, which tells the story of J. J. Thomson, Ernest Rutherford, and Thomson's son George Paget Thomson, who also won the Nobel Prize for his experiment that proved the existence of de Broglie's predicted electron waves.

Museums and Institutes

American Institute of Physics
Center for the History of Physics
One Physics Ellipse
College Park, MD 20740
(301) 209-3165
www.aip.org/history-programs/physics-history

The Center for History of Physics houses a research library, a photo archive, and has created numerous online resources in all areas of physics, including Rutherford's Nuclear World.

American Nuclear Society
555 North Kensington Avenue
La Grange Park, IL 60526
(800) 323-3044
www.ans.org

The American Nuclear Society is a not-for-profit, international, scientific and educational organization. It serves the nuclear community by promoting public awareness and understanding of the application of nuclear science and technology.

Ernest Rutherford Collection
Room 111 Ernest Rutherford Physics Building
McGill University
3600 rue University
Montréal, QC H3A 2T8
Canada
(514) 398-6490
www.mcgill.ca/historicalcollections/departmental/ernest-rutherford

The Rutherford Museum contains the apparatus used by Nobel Prize winner Ernest Rutherford when he was professor of experimental physics at McGill from 1898 to 1907. The collection includes letters, documents, memorabilia, photographs of Rutherford and his colleagues, and other materials relating to Rutherford's work, including the desk he used in his home.

Lederman Science Education Center
Fermilab MS 777
Box 500
Batavia, IL 60510
(630) 840-8258
ed.fnal.gov/lsc/lscvideo/index.shtml

This museum is an outstanding place to discover the science and history of subatomic particles. It is located at the Fermi National Accelerator Laboratory (Fermilab) outside of Chicago.

Ontario Science Centre
770 Don Mills Road
Toronto, ON M3C 1T3
Canada
(416) 696-1000
www.ontariosciencecentre.ca

The Ontario Science Centre is Canada's leading science and technology museum. Its programs and exhibits aim to inspire a lifelong journey of curiosity, discovery, and action to create a better future for the planet.

Index

Page numbers in **boldface** are illustrations. Entries in **boldface** are glossary terms.

About the Authors

Science educator and consultant **B. H. Fields** has worked behind the scenes in the publishing industry since the mid-1980s, specializing in books and articles on the physical sciences and technology for middle grades.

Award-winning children's author **Fred Bortz** spent the first twenty-five years of his working career as a physicist, gaining experience in fields as varied as nuclear reactor design, automobile engine control systems, and science education. He earned his PhD at Carnegie Mellon University, where he also worked in several research groups from 1979 through 1994. He has been a full-time writer since 1996.